Royal
Horticultural
Society

Sharing the best in Gardening

A GARDENER'S
FIVE YEAR
RECORD BOOK

F

FRANCES LINCOLN LIMITED

PUBLISHERS

Frances Lincoln Limited
www.franceslincoln.com

The Royal Horticultural Society A Gardener's Five Year Record Book
Copyright © Frances Lincoln Limited 2013
Text and illustrations copyright © the Royal Horticultural Society 2013
and printed under licence granted by the Royal Horticultural Society,
Registered Charity number 222879/SC038262.
For more information visit our website or call 0845 130 4646
An interest in gardening is all you need to enjoy being a member
of the RHS.
Website: www.rhs.org.uk

First Frances Lincoln edition 2013

A catalogue record for this book is available from the British Library

Designed by Arianna Osti

ISBN: 978-0-7112-3417-8

Printed in China

9 8 7 6 5 4 3 2 1

FRONT COVER A sweet pea, *Lathyrus odoratus*, watercolour on vellum by
Georg Dionysius Ehret (1708–70), dated 1757; 'Anemones', cultivars of
Anemone coronaria: watercolour on vellum by James Bolton (c.1735–99),
dated 1791.
BACK COVER The coral tree, *Erythrina coralloides*: watercolour on vellum
by Eliza Smith (*fl.*1780s), dated 1785.
TITLE PAGE 'Monier's Passion Flower': watercolour on vellum by
James Bolton (c.1735–99). It resembles *P. × alato-caerulea* (now *P. ×
belotii*), which was named in 1824; could it have been an early hybrid?
RIGHT Wolfsbane, *Aconitum napellus*: watercolour on vellum by
Pierre Jean François Turpin (1775–1840).

RHS Flower Show information
Can be found by visiting www.rhs.org.uk or telephoning the 24-hour
Flower Show Information Line (020 7649 1885)

INTRODUCTION

THE ILLUSTRATIONS in this book have been taken from works of art on vellum held in the collection of the RHS Lindley Library. Vellum, like parchment, was made from the skin of sheep, goat or calf, but specially prepared by scraping and rubbing. It has been extensively used by artists as a medium for drawing. Paintings on vellum have a luminosity and richness that is quite unlike those on paper.

The oldest collection of drawings on vellum in the RHS collection is Italian in provenance, unattributed and undated. The drawings have been considered as 17th-century work but evidence suggests they may be early 18th century instead. Other works included here are from an album of six drawings by Claude Aubriet (1665–1742), which could have been compiled any time in the opening decades of the 18th century. Aubriet used a mixture of watercolour and body colour – an unstable combination as the pigment becomes brittle with age and can flake off.

Georg Dionysius Ehret (1708–70) was the most eminent botanical artist of the mid-18th century. Although most of his work was on paper he drew some large pieces on vellum. His use of vellum may have been dictated purely by its effect on colour.

James Bolton (c.1735–99) is remembered today as the author of pioneering books on the ferns and fungi of Britain.

Margaret Meen (fl.1775–1806) exhibited at the Royal Academy in the 1770s and 1780s. Her drawings are purely plant portraits.

Margaret Meen also taught drawing to others, including the four daughters of Joshua Smith, the Member of Parliament for Devizes (Emma, Eliza or Elizabeth, Augusta and Maria). Works by all four are included here and date from the 1780s.

The latest artist represented here is Pierre Jean François Turpin (1775–1840), an artist famous for the almost microscopic detail he put into his drawings. In 1820 Turpin and Pierre Antoine Poiteau (1766–1854) published a work on plant anatomy and taxonomy called *Leçons de Flore*, and two copies of this work were specially printed on vellum, and the prints hand-coloured by Turpin.

Today, there has been a revival of interest in vellum and this book gives a taste of the legacy of their predecessors.

Brent Elliott
Historian, RHS Lindley Library

YEAR		
WEATHER		
PLANTS IN BLOOM		
TASKS		
NOTES		

A black hellebore, *Helleborus niger*: coloured illustration on vellum by Pierre Jean François Turpin (1775–1840) from *Leçons de Flore* (1820).

JANUARY

YEAR

WEATHER

PLANTS IN
BLOOM

TASKS

NOTES

Narcissus pseudonarcissus: watercolour on
vellum by an anonymous Italian artist, 17th or
early 18th century.

JANUARY

YEAR

WEATHER

PLANTS IN
BLOOM

TASKS

NOTES

Lilium martagon: watercolour on vellum by an
anonymous Italian artist, 17th or early 18th century.

JANUARY

YEAR		
WEATHER		
PLANTS IN BLOOM		
TASKS		
NOTES		

The Virgin's bower, *Clematis viticella*: watercolour
on vellum by Emma Smith (*fl.*1780s–1845).

JANUARY

YEAR		
WEATHER		
PLANTS IN BLOOM		
TASKS		
NOTES		

Narcissus tazetta: watercolour on vellum by an anonymous Italian artist, 17th or early 18th century.

JANUARY

YEAR		
WEATHER		
PLANTS IN BLOOM		
TASKS		
NOTES		

Iris foetidissima: watercolour on vellum by an anonymous Italian artist, 17th or early 18th century.

FEBRUARY

YEAR

WEATHER

PLANTS IN
BLOOM

TASKS

NOTES

Two tulip cultivars: watercolour on vellum by an
anonymous Italian artist, 17th or early 18th century.

FEBRUARY

YEAR

WEATHER

PLANTS IN
BLOOM

TASKS

NOTES

The Guernsey lily, *Nerine sarniensis*: watercolour
on vellum by Eliza Smith (*fl.*1780s).

FEBRUARY

YEAR		
WEATHER		
PLANTS IN BLOOM		
TASKS		
NOTES		

From left to right, *Narcissus tazetta* and *Narcissus cantabricus*: watercolour on vellum by an anonymous Italian artist, 17th or early 18th century.

FEBRUARY

YEAR		
WEATHER		
PLANTS IN BLOOM		
TASKS		
NOTES		

Camellia japonica: watercolour on vellum
by Margaret Meen (*fl*.1775–1806), dated 1789.

FEBRUARY

YEAR

WEATHER

PLANTS IN
BLOOM

TASKS

NOTES

A dog's-tooth violet, *Erythronium dens-canis*:
watercolour on vellum by James Bolton (*c*.1735–99).

MARCH

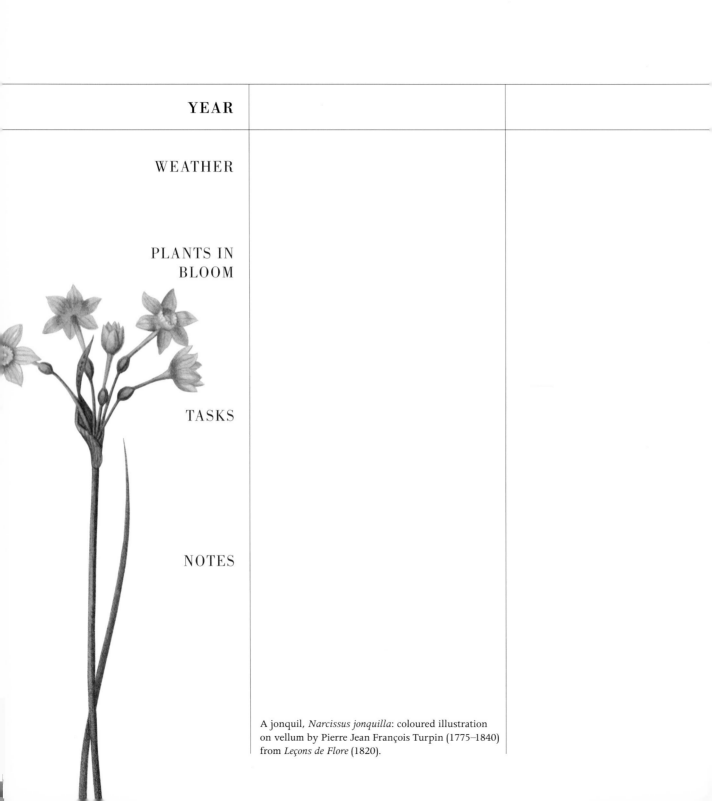

YEAR

WEATHER

PLANTS IN
BLOOM

TASKS

NOTES

A jonquil, *Narcissus jonquilla*: coloured illustration
on vellum by Pierre Jean François Turpin (1775–1840)
from *Leçons de Flore* (1820).

MARCH

YEAR		
WEATHER		
PLANTS IN BLOOM		
TASKS		
NOTES		

The lady tulip, *Tulipa clusiana*: watercolour on vellum by an anonymous Italian artist, 17th or early 18th century.

MARCH

YEAR		
WEATHER		
PLANTS IN BLOOM		
TASKS		

The Chinese flowering apple, formerly *Pyrus spectabilis*, now *Malus spectabilis*: watercolour on vellum by Eliza Smith (*fl.*1780s), dated 1788.

MARCH

YEAR		
WEATHER		
PLANTS IN BLOOM		
TASKS		
NOTES		

Narcissus tazetta: watercolour on vellum by an anonymous Italian artist, 17th or early 18th century.

MARCH

YEAR		
WEATHER		
PLANTS IN BLOOM		
TASKS		
NOTES		

A cultivar of *Anemone coronaria*: watercolour on vellum by an anonymous Italian artist, 17th or early 18th century.

APRIL

YEAR		
WEATHER		
PLANTS IN BLOOM		
TASKS		

The passion flower, *Passiflora laurifolia*:
watercolour on vellum by Margaret Meen
(*fl.*1775–1806), dated 1785.

APRIL

YEAR

WEATHER

PLANTS IN
BLOOM

TASKS

NOTES

An elaborate but unnamed cultivar of *Anemone coronaria*: watercolour on vellum by an anonymous Italian artist, 17th or early 18th century.

APRIL

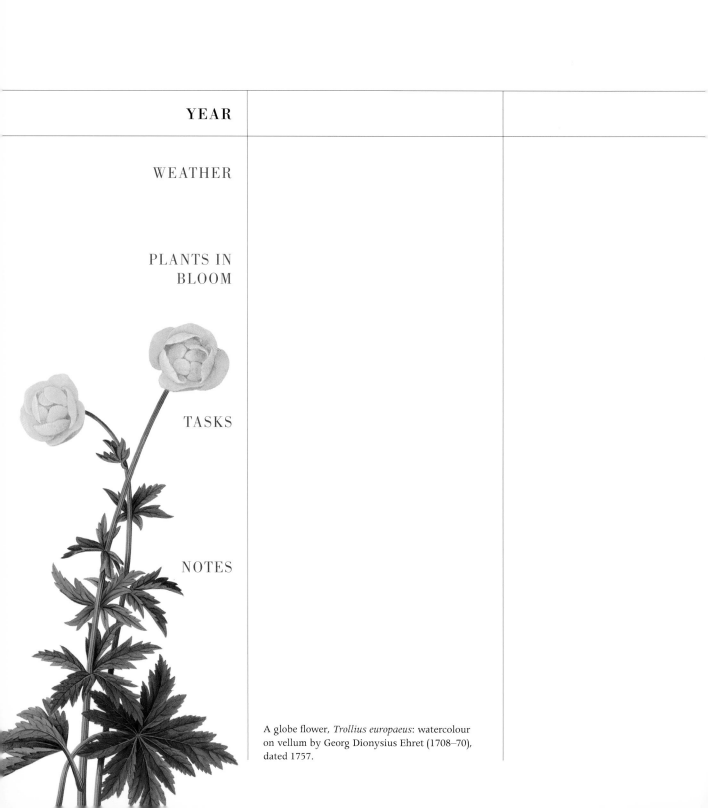

YEAR

WEATHER

PLANTS IN
BLOOM

TASKS

NOTES

A globe flower, *Trollius europaeus*: watercolour
on vellum by Georg Dionysius Ehret (1708–70),
dated 1757.

APRIL

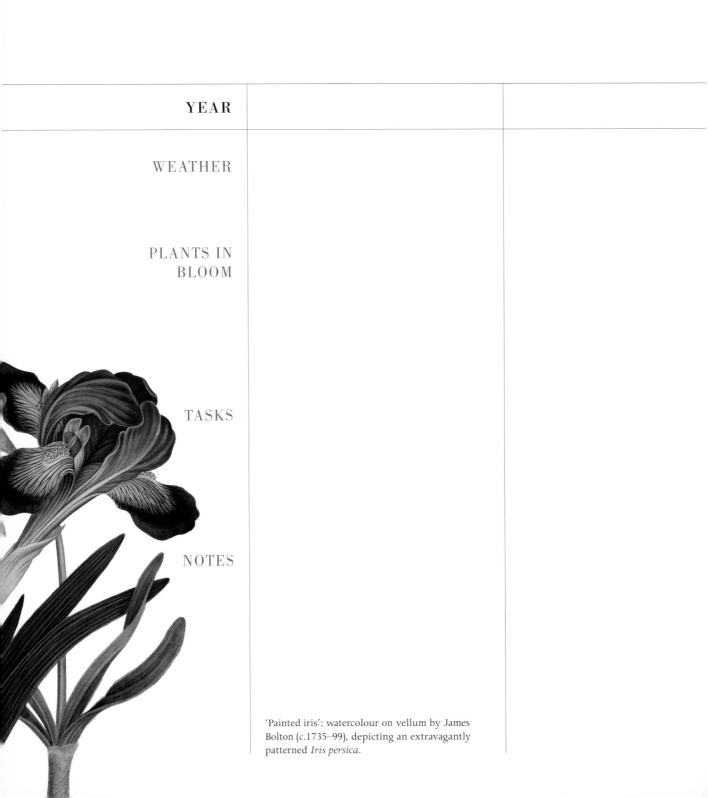

YEAR		
WEATHER		
PLANTS IN BLOOM		
TASKS		
NOTES		

'Painted iris': watercolour on vellum by James Bolton (c.1735–99), depicting an extravagantly patterned *Iris persica*.

APRIL

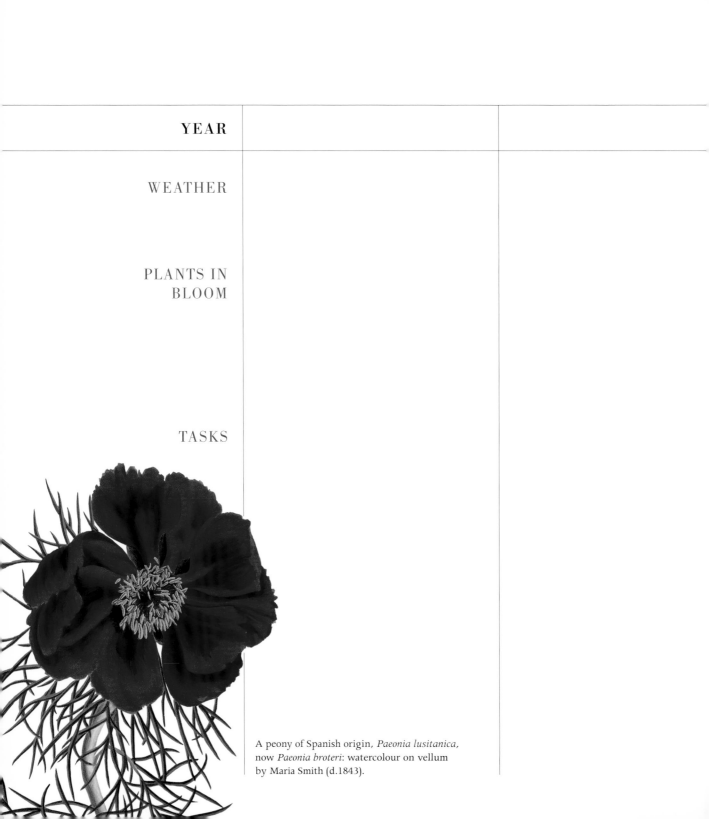

YEAR		
WEATHER		
PLANTS IN BLOOM		
TASKS		

A peony of Spanish origin, *Paeonia lusitanica*,
now *Paeonia broteri*: watercolour on vellum
by Maria Smith (d.1843).

MAY

YEAR

WEATHER

PLANTS IN
BLOOM

TASKS

NOTES

The silky stewartia, *Stewartia malacodendron*:
watercolour on vellum by James Bolton (*c*.1735–99).

MAY

YEAR

WEATHER

PLANTS IN
BLOOM

TASKS

NOTES

A cultivar of *Anemone coronaria,* showing proliferation:
watercolour on vellum by an anonymous Italian artist,
17th or early 18th century.

MAY

YEAR		
WEATHER		
PLANTS IN BLOOM		
TASKS		
NOTES		

Fuchsia coccinea: watercolour on vellum
by James Bolton (c.1735–99).

MAY

YEAR		
WEATHER		
PLANTS IN BLOOM		
TASKS		
NOTES		

Anemone coronaria 'Flore Pleno': watercolour on vellum by an anonymous Italian artist, 17th or early 18th century.

MAY

YEAR		
WEATHER		
PLANTS IN BLOOM		
TASKS		

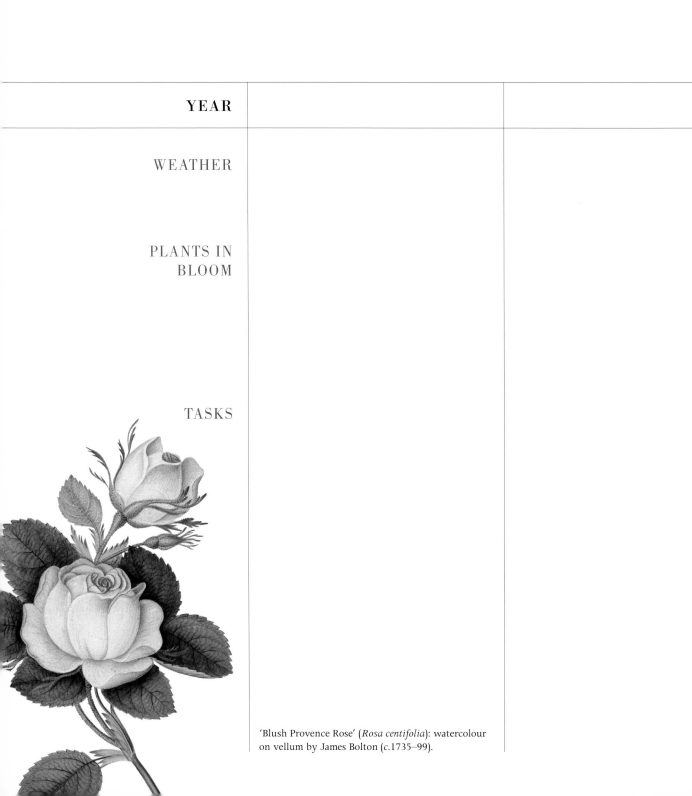

'Blush Provence Rose' (*Rosa centifolia*): watercolour on vellum by James Bolton (c.1735–99).

JUNE

YEAR

WEATHER

PLANTS IN
BLOOM

TASKS

NOTES

The globe flower, *Trollius europaeus*:
watercolour on vellum by Pierre Jean
François Turpin (1775–1840).

JUNE

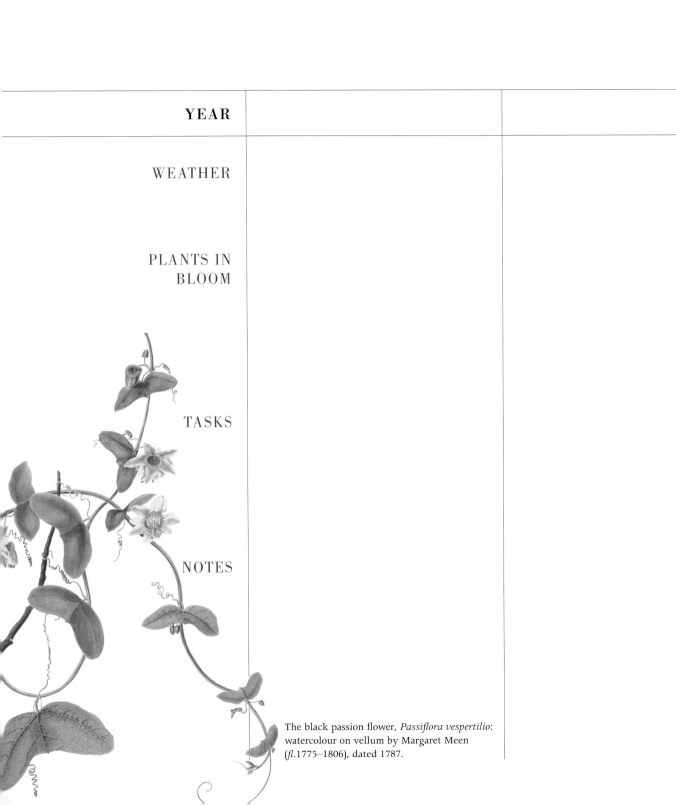

YEAR		
WEATHER		
PLANTS IN BLOOM		
TASKS		
NOTES		

The black passion flower, *Passiflora vespertilio*: watercolour on vellum by Margaret Meen (*fl.*1775–1806), dated 1787.

JUNE

YEAR

WEATHER

PLANTS IN
BLOOM

TASKS

NOTES

Wolfsbane, *Aconitum napellus*: watercolour on
vellum by Pierre Jean François Turpin (1775–1840).

JUNE

YEAR		
WEATHER		
PLANTS IN BLOOM		
TASKS		
NOTES		

The oleander, *Nerium oleander*: watercolour on vellum by Augusta Smith (*fl.*1780s–1845).

JUNE

YEAR		
WEATHER		
PLANTS IN BLOOM		
TASKS		
NOTES		

'A Balsam' (unnamed cultivar of *Impatiens balsamina*): watercolour on vellum by James Bolton (c.1735–99).

JULY

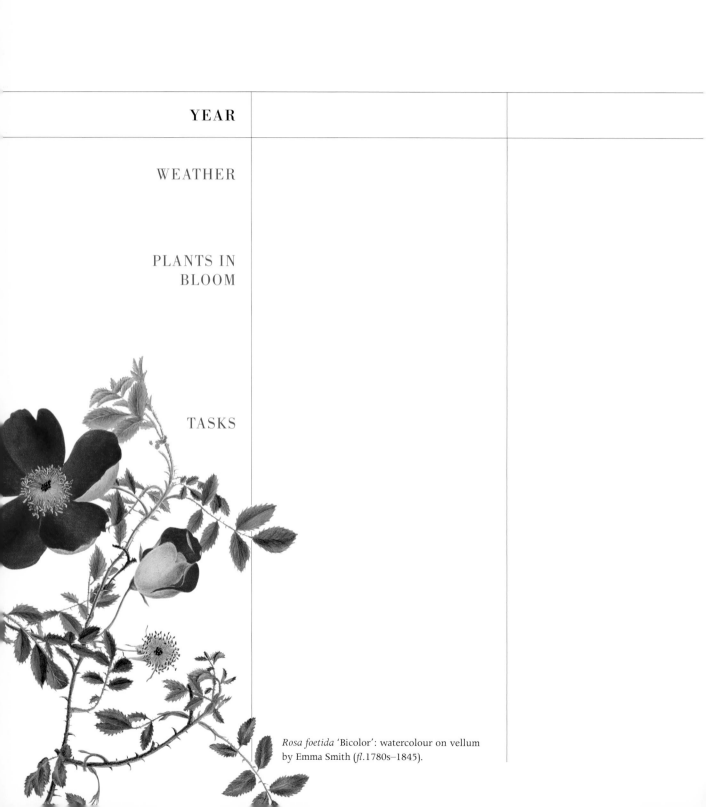

	YEAR		
WEATHER			
PLANTS IN BLOOM			
TASKS			

Rosa foetida 'Bicolor': watercolour on vellum by Emma Smith (*fl.*1780s–1845).

JULY

YEAR		
WEATHER		
PLANTS IN BLOOM		
TASKS		
NOTES		

A foxglove, possibly *Digitalis lanata*, introduced in 1789: watercolour on vellum by Eliza Smith (*fl.*1780s).

JULY

YEAR		
WEATHER		
PLANTS IN BLOOM		
TASKS		

The anatomy of fruits: coloured illustration on vellum by Pierre Jean François Turpin (1775–1840) from *Leçons de Flore* (1820).

JULY

YEAR		
WEATHER		
PLANTS IN BLOOM		
TASKS		
NOTES		

A larkspur, *Delphinium elatum*: watercolour on vellum by Margaret Meen (*fl*.1775–1806), dated 1785.

JULY

YEAR

WEATHER

PLANTS IN
BLOOM

TASKS

NOTES

Lilium bulbiferum: watercolour on vellum
by an anonymous Italian artist, 17th or early
18th century.

AUGUST

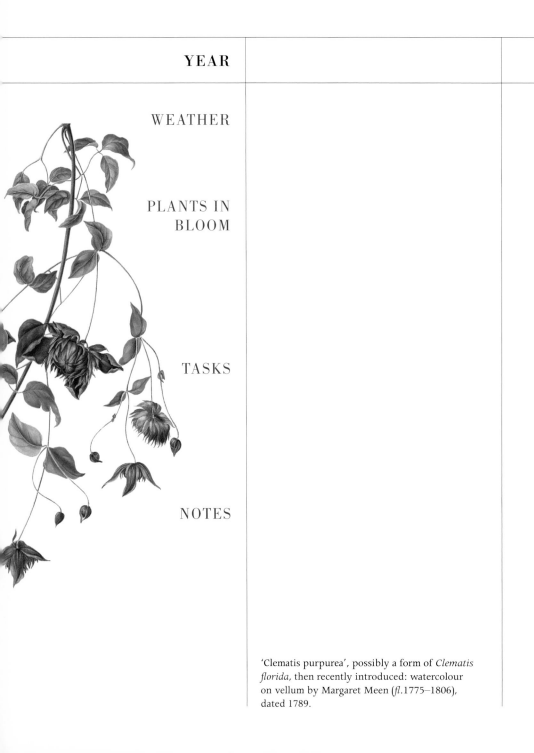

YEAR		
WEATHER		
PLANTS IN BLOOM		
TASKS		
NOTES		

'Clematis purpurea', possibly a form of *Clematis florida*, then recently introduced: watercolour on vellum by Margaret Meen (*fl.*1775–1806), dated 1789.

AUGUST

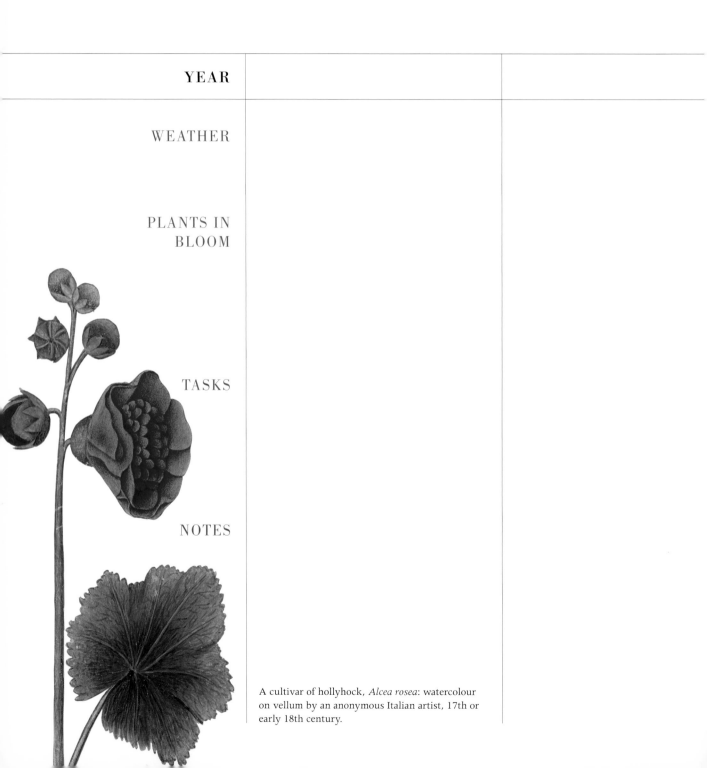

YEAR

WEATHER

PLANTS IN
BLOOM

TASKS

NOTES

A cultivar of hollyhock, *Alcea rosea*: watercolour
on vellum by an anonymous Italian artist, 17th or
early 18th century.

AUGUST

YEAR		
WEATHER		
PLANTS IN BLOOM		
TASKS		
NOTES		

'Vinca rosea, White Madagascar Periwinkle',
watercolour on vellum by James Bolton (*c*.1735–99),
depicting plants grown in the hothouse at Fixby
Hall near Huddersfield.

AUGUST

YEAR		
WEATHER		
PLANTS IN BLOOM		
TASKS		
NOTES		

The anatomy of fruits: coloured illustration on vellum by Pierre Jean François Turpin (1775–1840) from *Leçons de Flore* (1820).

AUGUST

YEAR		
WEATHER		
PLANTS IN BLOOM		
TASKS		
NOTES		

The Turkcap or Turk's turban, *Malvaviscus arboreus*:
watercolour on vellum by Eliza Smith (*fl.*1780s).

SEPTEMBER

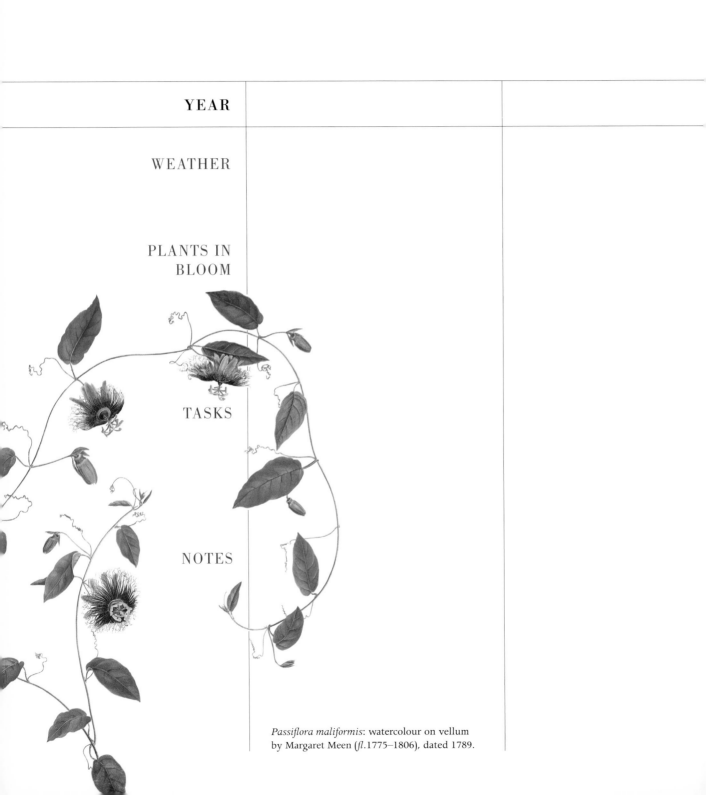

YEAR

WEATHER

PLANTS IN
BLOOM

TASKS

NOTES

Passiflora maliformis: watercolour on vellum
by Margaret Meen (*fl.*1775–1806), dated 1789.

SEPTEMBER

YEAR		
WEATHER		
PLANTS IN BLOOM		
TASKS		

The Spanish flag, *Lantana camara*: watercolour
on vellum by Eliza Smith (*fl*.1780s).

SEPTEMBER

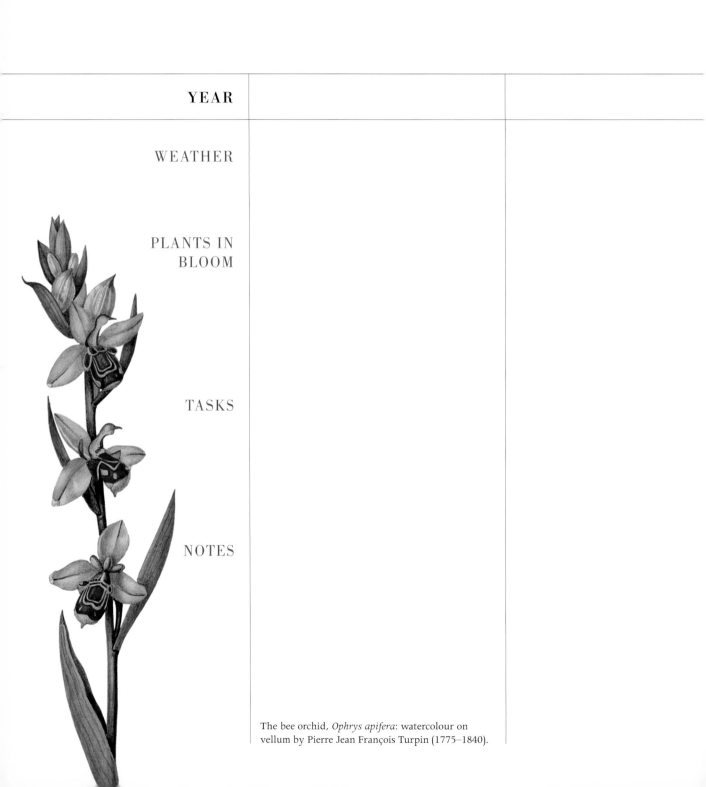

YEAR		
WEATHER		
PLANTS IN BLOOM		
TASKS		
NOTES		

The bee orchid, *Ophrys apifera*: watercolour on
vellum by Pierre Jean François Turpin (1775–1840).

SEPTEMBER

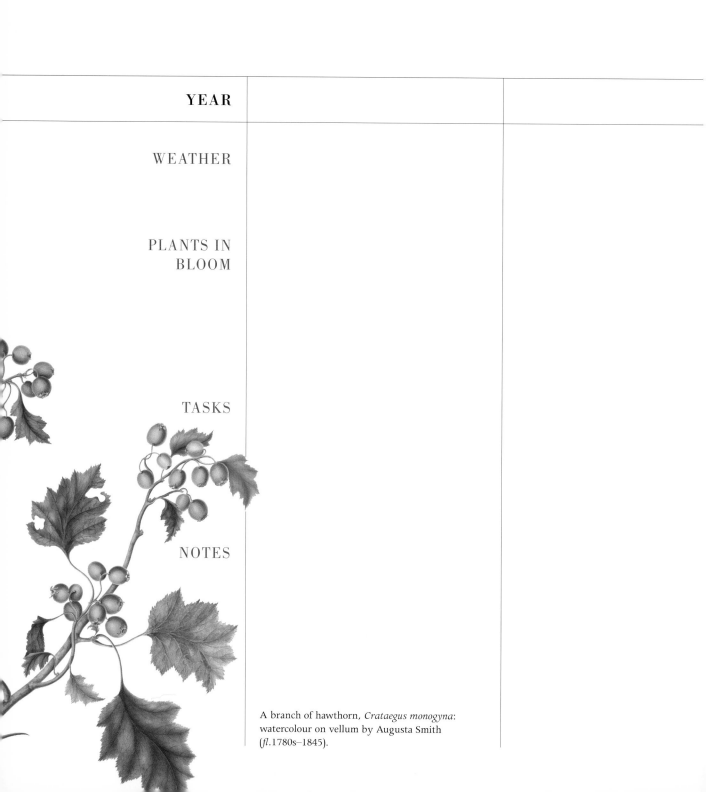

YEAR		
WEATHER		
PLANTS IN BLOOM		
TASKS		
NOTES		

A branch of hawthorn, *Crataegus monogyna*: watercolour on vellum by Augusta Smith (*fl.*1780s–1845).

SEPTEMBER

YEAR

WEATHER

PLANTS IN
BLOOM

TASKS

'Bignonia', *Campsis radicans*: watercolour
on vellum by Margaret Meen (*fl.*1775–1806),
dated 1785.

OCTOBER

YEAR		
WEATHER		
PLANTS IN BLOOM		
TASKS		
NOTES		

The strawberry tree, *Arbutus unedo*: watercolour on vellum by Margaret Meen (*fl.*1775–1806), dated 1784.

OCTOBER

YEAR		
WEATHER		
PLANTS IN BLOOM		
TASKS		
NOTES		

The anatomy of fruits: coloured illustration on vellum by Pierre Jean François Turpin (1775–1840) from *Leçons de Flore* (1820).

OCTOBER

YEAR		
WEATHER		
PLANTS IN BLOOM		
TASKS		
NOTES		

The Carolina allspice, *Calycanthus floridus*:
watercolour on vellum by Eliza Smith (*fl*.1780s).

OCTOBER

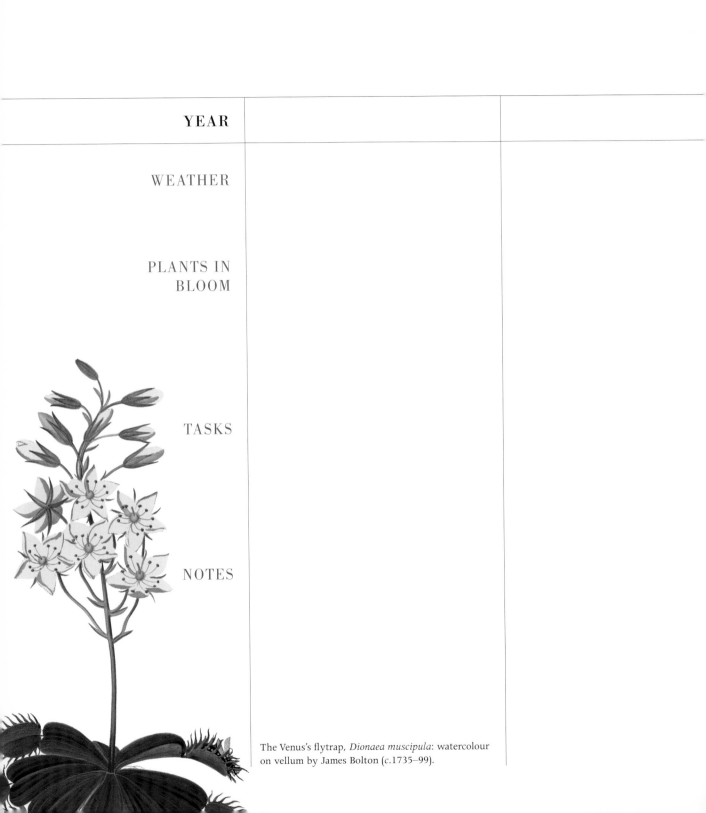

YEAR		
WEATHER		
PLANTS IN BLOOM		
TASKS		
NOTES		

The Venus's flytrap, *Dionaea muscipula*: watercolour on vellum by James Bolton (*c.*1735–99).

OCTOBER

YEAR		
WEATHER		
PLANTS IN BLOOM		
TASKS		
NOTES		

'Jacobean lily', *Sprekelia formosissima*: watercolour on vellum by James Bolton (*c*.1735–99).

NOVEMBER

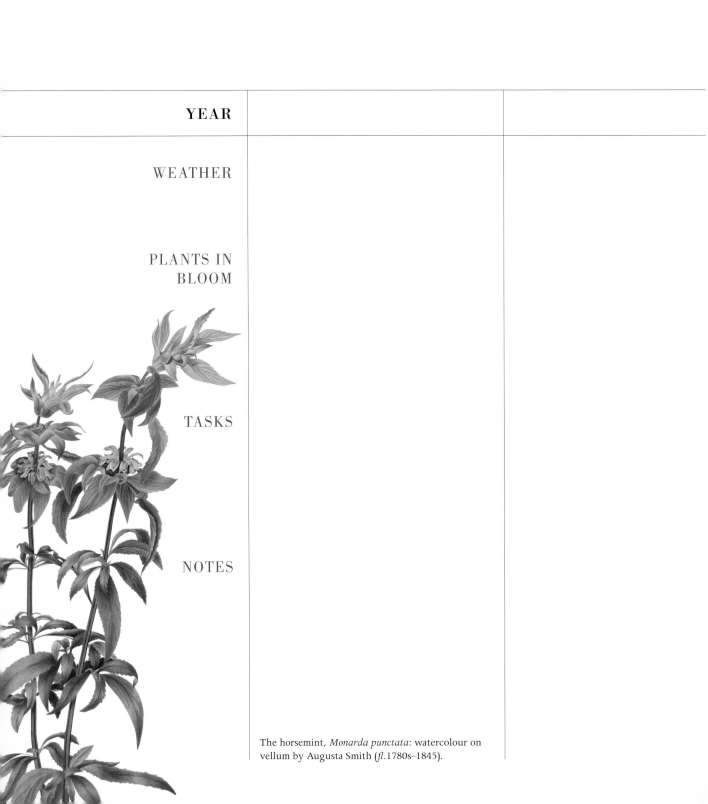

YEAR

WEATHER

PLANTS IN
BLOOM

TASKS

NOTES

The horsemint, *Monarda punctata*: watercolour on
vellum by Augusta Smith (*fl*.1780s–1845).

NOVEMBER

	YEAR	
WEATHER		
PLANTS IN BLOOM		
TASKS		
NOTES		

The pomegranate, *Punica granatum*: watercolour and body colour on vellum by Claude Aubriet (1665–1742).

NOVEMBER

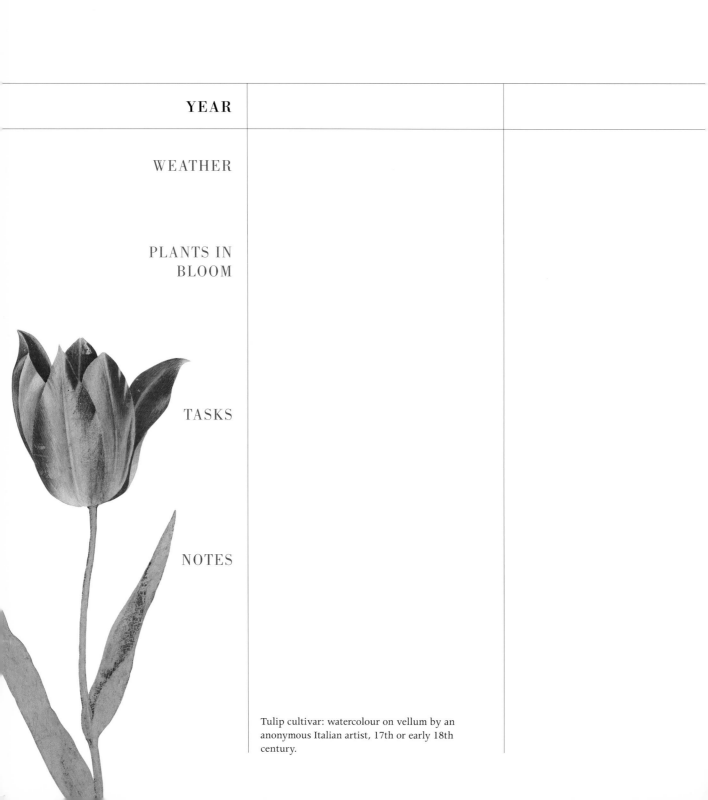

YEAR

WEATHER

PLANTS IN
BLOOM

TASKS

NOTES

Tulip cultivar: watercolour on vellum by an
anonymous Italian artist, 17th or early 18th
century.

NOVEMBER

YEAR		
WEATHER		
PLANTS IN BLOOM		
TASKS		
NOTES		

The marsh marigold, *Caltha palustris*:
watercolour on vellum by Pierre Jean
François Turpin (1775–1840).

NOVEMBER

YEAR

WEATHER

PLANTS IN
BLOOM

TASKS

A turban lily, *Lilium pomponium*: watercolour
on vellum by an anonymous Italian artist, 17th
or early 18th century.

DECEMBER

YEAR		
WEATHER		
PLANTS IN BLOOM		
TASKS		
NOTES		

'Bignonia echinata, Hedge-hog Trumpet Flower',
now *Amphilophium crucigerum*: watercolour on
vellum by James Bolton (*c*.1735–99).

DECEMBER

YEAR		
WEATHER		
PLANTS IN BLOOM		
TASKS		
NOTES		

Yellow archangel, *Galeopsis galeobdalon*:
watercolour on vellum by Georg Dionysius
Ehret (1708–70), dated 1757.

DECEMBER

YEAR		
WEATHER		
PLANTS IN BLOOM		
TASKS		
NOTES		

A *Hippeastrum reginae*: watercolour on vellum by an anonymous Italian artist, 17th or early 18th century.

DECEMBER

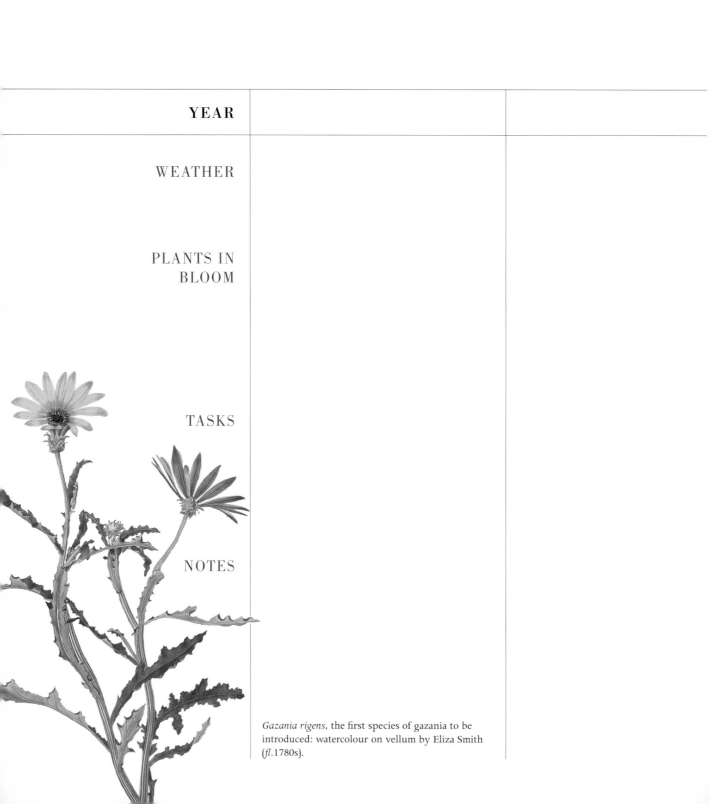

YEAR

WEATHER

PLANTS IN
BLOOM

TASKS

NOTES

Gazania rigens, the first species of gazania to be
introduced: watercolour on vellum by Eliza Smith
(*fl*.1780s).

DECEMBER

PLANTS TO BUY

PLANT NAME	WHERE SEEN	SUPPLIER	PLANTING POSIT

PLANTS TO BUY

PLANT NAME	WHERE SEEN	SUPPLIER	PLANTING POSITION

PLANTS TO BUY

PLANT NAME	WHERE SEEN	SUPPLIER	PLANTING POSIT

PLANTS TO BUY

PLANT NAME	WHERE SEEN	SUPPLIER	PLANTING POSITION

PLANT SUPPLIERS

NAME	USEFUL ADDRESSES	TEL/EMAIL

PLANT SUPPLIERS

NAME	USEFUL ADDRESSES	TEL/EMAIL

PLANT SUPPLIERS

NAME	USEFUL ADDRESSES	TEL/EMAIL

PLANT SUPPLIERS

NAME	USEFUL ADDRESSES	TEL/EMAIL

GARDENS TO VISIT

GARDEN	WHEN TO VISIT	LOOK FOR

GARDENS TO VISIT

DATE VISITED	COMMENTS

GARDENS TO VISIT

GARDEN	WHEN TO VISIT	LOOK FOR

GARDENS TO VISIT

DATE VISITED	COMMENTS

NOTES